LOTUS

SPEED MACHINES

Julia J. Quinlan

PowerKiDS press

New York

Published in 2014 by The Rosen Publishing Group, Inc.
29 East 21st Street, New York, NY 10010

First Edition

Editor: Jennifer Way
Book Design: Greg Tucker
Book Layout: Kate Vlachos

Photo Credits: Cover © Uli Jooss/culture-ima/age fotostock; p. 5 Maksim Toome/Shutterstock.com; p. 6 Central Pass/Stringer/Hulton Archive/Getty Images; pp. 7, 19 Miguel Medina/Stringer/AFP/Getty Images; pp. 8, 25 (top), 25 (bottom) Bloomberg/Getty Images; p. 9 citybrabus/Shutterstock.com; p. 10 Teerapun/Shutterstock.com; p. 11 (top) Peter Scholz/Shutterstock.com; p. 11 (bottom) Gert Vrey/Shutterstock.com; p. 13 Paul Gilham/Getty Images Sport/Getty Images; p. 14 © AP Images; p. 15 Robert Riger/Getty Images Sport/Getty Images; p. 17 Gertan/Shutterstock.com; p. 18 Oli Scarff/Getty Images New/Getty Images; p. 21 RacingOne/ISC Archives/Getty Images; p. 22 foto76/Shutterstock.com; p. 23 NizamD/Shutterstock.com; p. 24 TachePhoto/Shutterstock.com; p. 26 esbobeldijk/Shutterstock.com; p. 27 S. Borisov/Shutterstock.com; pp. 28–29 NorGal/Shutterstock.com.

Library of Congress Cataloging-in-Publication Data

Quinlan, Julia J.
  Lotus / By Julia J. Quinlan. — First edition.
      pages cm
  Includes index.
  ISBN 978-1-4777-0805-7 (library binding) — ISBN 978-1-4777-0984-9 (pbk.) —
ISBN 978-1-4777-0985-6 (6-pack)
  1. Lotus automobiles—Juvenile literature. I. Title.
  TL215.L67Q56 2014
  629.222'2—dc23
                              2012042266

Manufactured in the United States of America

CPSIA Compliance Information: Batch #S13PK8: For Further Information contact Rosen Publishing, New York, New York at 1-800-237-9932

Contents

Born in Britain

Lotus Cars is a British sports car and racecar company. Founded in 1952, Lotus is known for its powerful but lightweight automobiles. Lotus sports cars are stylish and eye-catching. They are **aerodynamic**, with narrow fronts and wider backs. They are built to have the handling and control of racecars. Besides making beautiful sports cars, Lotus is also known for its excellence in **engineering**. Lotus has made many **innovations** in car and engine construction. Lotus has engineered not only its own cars but also cars for other companies, such as Jaguar and Aston Martin.

Lotus has been making beautiful luxury sports cars for a long time. However, Lotus started as a racecar company and did not have any interest in making sports cars. The company began making sports cars only to fund its racecars and racing team!

The Lotus Exige S has been produced since 2005. Its design was based on the Lotus Elise, an earlier model.

Colin Chapman founded Lotus in 1952. Chapman studied engineering in college but had a passion for racing. Before making his own cars, he modified, or made changes to, other company's cars. In 1948, he modified a 1928 Austin Seven and called it the Lotus Mark I. In 1949, he modified another Austin Seven and called it the Lotus Mark II. In 1952, Chapman founded the Lotus Engineering Company.

Colin Chapman

The Lotus Elite is a model that will be relaunched in 2014. Here is a concept model, or sample version, of that model at the 2010 Paris Motor Show.

In 1957, Lotus made its first **production** car, the Lotus Elite. A production car is made and sold to the public, rather than made to be a racecar. Chapman built the car in hopes that he could use money from car sales to fund his racing team and to keep building racecars. Even though Lotus's focus was on racing, its sports car was a hit. Chapman died in 1982. After Chapman's death, Lotus was sold to General Motors in 1986. General Motors later sold Lotus to a Malaysian company, Proton.

Lightweight Power

Lotus is known for its innovative engineering. One of Lotus's most famous goals is to make its cars as light as possible. Lighter cars go faster more easily than heavier cars. A lighter car also tends to have better **fuel efficiency** because less energy is required to make it move than a heavier car. The more fuel-efficient a car is, the longer it can drive without needing more gas.

Sports cars, such as this Lotus Exige, are often described as aerodynamic. That means that the car can move quickly because the force of air moving around it is reduced by the car's design.

Like many other high-performance sports cars, Lotuses sit low to the ground. This makes a car more aerodynamic. The model shown here is a 2012 Lotus Evora.

Lotuses are designed to be aerodynamic, which is another part of the design that makes them fast cars. In 1962, Lotus made the Type 25, which was the first car with a **monocoque chassis**. The chassis is the internal frame of the car. A monocoque chassis means that the body and chassis are one piece. In 1981, the Lotus Type 88 became the first car with a monocoque chassis made from a lightweight material called carbon fiber. This innovation helped reduce the overall weight of the car.

Sports Cars

Lotus's focus has always been on making sports cars that drive like racecars. Lotus sports cars are not typically made for day-to-day life. Many companies make sports cars that are more practical. For example, they might be fast and handle well, but they will also have large trunks and seats for more than two people. Lotuses are not made for comfort or practicality. Lotuses are made for people who want a taste of the racecar experience while driving on the highway.

Here is a rear view of a Lotus Elise SC. The "SC" stands for "supercharged" because it is faster than other Elise models.

Above: This is a 1969 Lotus Elan convertible. *Right*: Here is a close-up look at a Lotus's headlights. Lotus headlights are inset so that they follow the curves of the car. This makes the cars aerodynamic.

The focus on creating a racecar-style sports car has been very successful for Lotus and has won it many fans. Its sports cars are fast and have very **precise** handling. Drivers can feel the road and effect of every turn or shift they make. This is partly because Lotuses are so lightweight.

Racecars

In 1954, Lotus officially became a racing team. The Mark 8 was the first model made by Lotus that was entered in international racing competitions. Lotus won its first 24 Hours of Le Mans in 1957, with the Lotus Eleven. The team won its first Formula One constructor's championship and driver's championship in 1963 with the Type 25. Lotus continued to innovate and engineer excellent racecars.

Even today, Lotus is still a competitive team in racing. For the 2012 season, the Lotus Formula One team raced the Lotus E20. The E20 has a V8 engine and a seven-speed semiautomatic **transmission**. A V8 engine means that the engine had 8 cylinders arranged in the shape of a V. Engines with more cylinders are more powerful. The E20 was designed at the team's headquarters in Enstone, England. It is the 20th model to be designed there, and the model's name comes from these two facts.

Here is a Lotus E20 in a Formula One race. The E20 has a semiautomatic transmission, which means that the driver shifts gears manually, but there is no clutch pedal, as there is in a manual transmission.

Racing

Lotus has been involved in different kinds of racing. Lotus began racing in Formula Two races in 1957 and shortly after moved up to Formula One. Formula One and Formula Two racing use the same types of cars. Formula One racing is one of the best racing competitions in the world, and Formula Two racing is one level below Formula One.

This photo shows a Lotus Eleven during a 1957 race. The Eleven was Lotus's most successful racecar design.

Here is a Lotus Formula One racecar in the mid-1960s.

Many other sports car companies, like Ferrari and Mercedes, have teams competing in Formula One. Lotus has won seven Formula One constructor's championships. The constructor is the company that designed and built the car. That can be different from the actual team. The team is usually named after the company that sponsors, or pays for, the car.

Many of Lotus's championships were a long time ago. The company started to become more active in racing again in the 2000s, competing in both Formula One and in Le Mans races.

Lotus Seven

The Lotus Seven was one of Lotus's best-known and most successful sports cars. The Lotus Seven was made from 1957 to 1972. Lotus founder Colin Chapman designed the Lotus Seven. Chapman wanted his cars to be lightweight and simple but have excellent performance. The Lotus Seven was seen as the perfect example of that.

The Lotus Seven was lightweight, simple, and powerful. You can still buy a Lotus Seven today, although they are no longer made by Lotus. In 1973, Lotus sold the production rights to Caterham, another British car company.

The Seven improved and changed over the years that it was in production. However, it maintained its basic styling. The Seven had a long front nose and a short back and was a two-seater sports car with the look of a racecar.

This is a 1970 Lotus Seven. This was the beginning of the fourth and final generation of Sevens that Lotus produced before selling the production rights to Caterham.

1957 Lotus Seven

Engine size	1.2 liters
Number of cylinders	4
Transmission	Manual
Gearbox	3 speeds
0–62 mph (0–100 km/h)	16 seconds
Top speed	80 mph (128 km/h)

Esprit

The Lotus Esprit was Lotus's first true supercar. Supercars are high-end, expensive, powerful sports cars. It was first shown as a concept car in 1972. A concept car is a car that is made to show new ideas and innovations. They are usually shown at car shows. The Esprit was put into production in 1976. Esprit was the first Lotus model that truly competed with Ferrari and Porsche in terms of styling and power. The Esprit was so popular that it was in production from 1976 to 2004. The Esprit was lightweight with precise handling, like all Lotus models.

Shown here is the white 1976 Lotus Esprit used in *The Spy Who Loved Me.*

1976 Esprit

Engine size	2.0 liters
Number of cylinders	4
Transmission	Manual
Gearbox	5 speeds
0–62 mph (0–100 km/h)	8.1 seconds
Top speed	124 mph (200 km/h)

The 2014 Lotus Esprit will kick off the sixth generation of this model.

The Esprit is also famous for appearing in the 1977 James Bond movie, *The Spy Who Loved Me*. In the movie, the Esprit could change into a submarine and travel underwater. That was just in the movie, though, not in real life!

The Lotus Elite was in production from 1957 to 1962. The Elite was also known as the Lotus Type 14. Colin Chapman always wanted to make his cars as lightweight as possible. The Elite was no exception. Unlike other brands of cars from this time period, the body of the Elite was made of fiberglass. Fiberglass is a plastic-like material that is made from very fine glass fibers. Fiberglass is much lighter than metals. The Elite weighed 1,510 pounds (685 kg). It was designed to look sleek and drive fast.

Because it was made of fiberglass, the Elite was also very long-lasting. Cars that are made of metal can rust and fall apart. Fiberglass does not rust. In fact, more than 600 of the 1,000 cars that were made are still around today!

Elite

Engine size	1.2 liters
Number of cylinders	4
Transmission	Manual
Gearbox	4 speeds
0–62 mph (0–100 km/h)	11.4 seconds
Top speed	112 mph (180 km/h)

A Lotus Elite (right) is competing against a Chevrolet Corvette in this 1962 race.

Elise

The Elise's body also helps the car have better braking and control. Here is a 2012 Lotus Elise at a car show.

Lotus debuted the Elise in 1996. It was a hit with car lovers when it first came out and is still being made today. The Elise is a two-seater with rear-wheel drive. This means that the rear wheels propel, or move, the car, and the front wheels do the steering. In a front-wheel drive, the front wheels both propel and steer the car. Many sports car drivers prefer the more precise handling of rear-wheel drive cars.

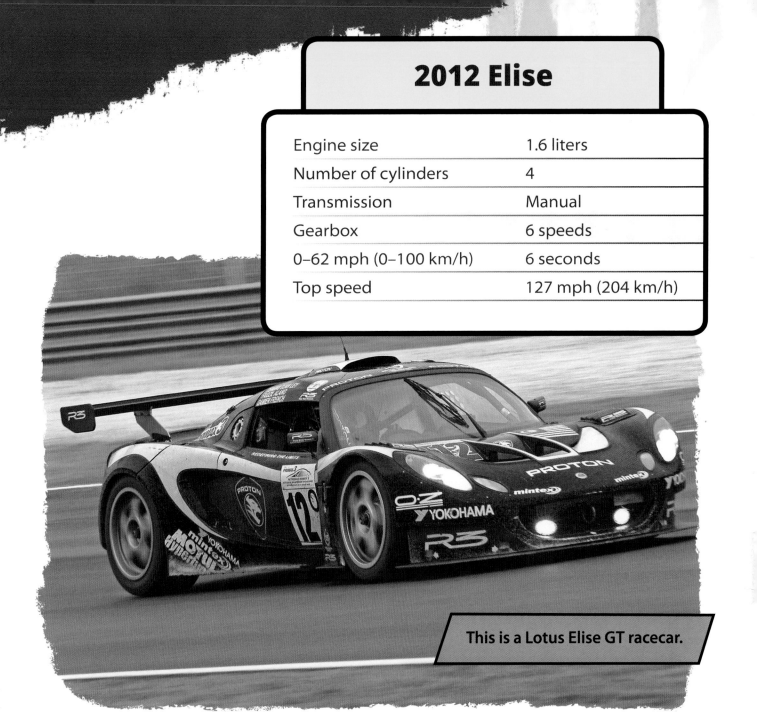

2012 Elise

Engine size	1.6 liters
Number of cylinders	4
Transmission	Manual
Gearbox	6 speeds
0–62 mph (0–100 km/h)	6 seconds
Top speed	127 mph (204 km/h)

This is a Lotus Elise GT racecar.

The Elise is aerodynamic and lightweight. Because the Elise is so light it has better fuel efficiency and lower **emission** levels than many other sports cars. A car with low emission levels lets out, or emits, lower amounts of harmful gases. Some gases made by cars can hurt the **environment** and cause **air pollution**. The Elise is simple in its construction, which makes it fast to manufacture. Since it is easy to put together, the Elise is more affordable than many other luxury sports cars.

Exige

2012 Exige S

Engine size	3.5 liters
Number of cylinders	6
Transmission	6 speeds
Gearbox	Manual
0–62 mph (0–100 km/h)	4 seconds
Top speed	170 mph (274 km/h)

The Lotus Exige is similar to the Lotus Elise. In fact, the body of the Exige is based on the body of the Elise. Lotus began production of the Exige in 2000. Like the Elise, the Exige is lightweight and sporty. The Exige has a rear spoiler, which the Elise does not. A rear spoiler is an attachment to the back of the car that makes the car more aerodynamic.

Here you can see the rear spoiler on this 2011 Lotus Exige.

Top: The Exige S has been available since 2005. Here is a dashboard view of this model. *Right*: The Lotus Exige S is shown here.

The Exige, like all Lotuses, is made for drivers who want to feel like they are racing around a track when they are driving down the street.

The Exige has the steering, control, and precision of a racecar. The 2012 Exige S is much faster than the Elise. It has a top speed of 170 mph (274 km/h) and 345 **horsepower**.

Evora

The Elise was the basis for both the Exige and the Europa S. The Europa S was made from 2006 until 2010. The Evora was the first originally designed model since the Elise. Every piece of the car was new and original. Lotus began production of the Evora in 2009.

Here is a racecar version of the Lotus Evora in a 2011 GT2 race.

2012 Evora

Engine size	3.5 liters
Number of cylinders	6
Transmission	Manual or automatic
Gearbox	6 speeds
0–62 mph (0–100 km/h)	4.8 seconds
Top speed	163 mph (262 km/h)

This is a 2012 Lotus Evora GTE. The company says that it is the most powerful Lotus it has produced to date.

The Evora is more practical than other Lotus models. It comes as a two-seater. There is also the option to have 2+2 seating. That means that there are two small seats in the back. With additional seats, the Evora can carry more than two passengers. Between its debut in 2009 and 2012, Lotus has made seven different racecars based on the Evora's design. It also makes the Evora GTE.

Lotus Now

In 2012, Lotus produced three car models. They were the Elise, the Exige, and the Evora. It might not sound like a lot, but each model has many options. For example, the Elise has three different options. There is the Elise, the Elise CR, and the Elise S. While all share the same basic design, the cars are different in their weight and power.

Even after Colin Chapman's death, Lotuses have been built with his ideas in mind. Lotuses are made to drive like racecars and to be lightweight and efficient. Lotuses continue to be among the most desirable luxury sports cars in the world. The company is smaller than its competitors, like Porsche and Ferrari, but it makes a huge statement anyway. Lotus has always innovated to remain at the forefront of the automobile industry.

This Lotus Elise is the convertible version of the model. Having lots of options allows buyers to customize their car and get exactly the style and performance they want.

Comparing Lotuses

CAR	YEARS MADE	SALES	TOP SPEED	FACT
Lotus Seven	1957–1973	1,900	80 mph (128 km/h)	The Lotus Seven, now made by Caterham, is the "oldest" new car you can buy today.
Esprit	1976–2004	10,675	124 mph (200 km/h)	Originally to be named Kiwi. But was changed to have an "e" name.
Elite	1957–1962	1,000	112 mph (180 km/h)	The racecar version of this model has won the 24 Hours of Le Mans six times.
Elise	1996–	n/a	127 mph (204 km/h)	Named after the granddaughter of Lotus chairman Romano Artioli.
Exige	2000–	n/a	170 mph (274 km/h)	The Exige is similar to the Elise but has a hardtop rather than a convertible top.
Evora	2009–	n/a	163 mph (262 km/h)	Two Evoras were donated to the Italian military police, called the Carabinieri.

Glossary

aerodynamic (er-oh-dy-NA-mik) Made to move through the air easily.

air pollution (AYR puh-LOO-shun) Harmful particles in the air.

emission (ee-MIH-shun) Something, such as pollution or gases, put into the air by something, such as an engine.

engineering (en-juh-NEER-ing) Making and using technology.

environment (en-VY-ern-ment) Everything that surrounds human beings and other organisms and everything that makes it possible for them to live.

fuel efficiency (FYOOL ih-FIH-shun-see) A measure of how well a car uses fuel.

horsepower (HORS-pow-er) The way an engine's power is measured. One horsepower is the power to lift 550 pounds (250 kg) 1 foot (.3 m) in 1 second.

innovations (ih-nuh-VAY-shuns) New ideas or methods to create things.

monocoque chassis (mon-uh-KOK CHA-see) A type of chassis in which the chassis and the body are one piece.

precise (prih-SYS) Exact.

production (pruh-DUK-shun) Made to sell.

transmission (trans-MIH-shun) A group of parts that includes the gears for changing speeds and that conveys the power from the engine to the machine's rear wheel.

Index

Websites

Due to the changing nature of Internet links, PowerKids Press has developed an online list of websites related to the subject of this book. This site is updated regularly. Please use this link to access the list: www.powerkidslinks.com/smach/lotus/